In My Mother's Footsteps

In My Mother's Footsteps

My Life and Experiences as a Hospice Nurse

DOROTHY WOODRUM

Inspiring Voices®

A Service of **Guideposts**

Inspiring Voices books may be ordered through booksellers or by contacting:

Inspiring Voices
1663 Liberty Drive
Bloomington, IN 47403
www.inspiringvoices.com
1-(866) 697-5313

ISBN: 978-1-4624-0508-4 (sc)
ISBN: 978-1-4624-0509-1 (hc)
ISBN: 978-1-4624-0507-7 (e)
Library of Congress Control Number: 2013901106

Printed in the United States of America

Inspiring Voices rev. date: 2/14/2013

This book is dedicated

to the memory of my mother, Rose Alma Gagne,

and to my children, Paul Glenn and Rose Alma,

who have been my life and joy.

Acknowledgments

I want to first give recognition to my Lord and Savior, Jesus Christ. Without him, I could not have done this.

To my grandchildren and great grandchildren: May God find in you faith and faithfulness so He may add your name in the Book of Life.

Thanks to my special friend and sister in Christ, Dionne Eichelberg, for her tireless effort to help edit and advise and her constant encouragement to write my legacy.

Thanks also to JoAnne Welman, Suzane Brown, and Amelia Aakers for encouraging me and telling me to write about my life and my experiences as a hospice nurse.

Preface

I am very happy in Christ that I have devoted my life to Him, my family, my friends, and of course my little dog, Monty.

This is my calling: to be on a mission for God until he returns.

I want to leave a legacy for all to remember me for what I have done for others, what they have meant to me, and how they have touched my life.

In My Mother's Footsteps is part of that legacy.

Introduction

My name is Dorothy Woodrum. My family and friends call me Dottie. As a hospice nurse for thirty-six years, I have had a lot of experience with terminally ill patients who had a short time to live. This is my story of my life and the extraordinary people whom I have cared for and become close to.

This book is dedicated to those who have blessed my life by allowing me to love and care for them and help prepare them in their final weeks—or days or sometimes hours—to meet their Lord and Savior as they leave this world for their final resting place.

Every champion in this life has a time when his or her life will come to an end. When that time comes, It's okay to rest. When our time is over in this life, our bodies rest until Jesus comes back and raises our bodies from their slumber in our graves to join up with our spirits in the air.

"For if we believe that Jesus died and rose again, even so them which are asleep in Jesus will God bring with him," says 1 Thessalonians 4 :14. Verses 16 and 17 tell how our bodies will become immortal instantly when they rise to join up with Jesus in the air.

Sometimes dying patients are fearful of the unknown. I share with them that when our hearts are right with God and we accept him as Savior, our spirits leave our bodies to be with Jesus. We graduate to our eternal home in heaven, and there our spirits never die. I reassure them they have nothing to fear. We comfort one another with these words.

Most of us want to have a goal in our lives. Mine is to make people happy. And I do. God has placed it in my heart to serve the sick and the dying. I know people feel the love of God in me, and I owe it all to the Holy Spirit, who guides me in all I do by placing me in the right places at the right times. I'm just an earthly vessel.

✚
Chapter 1

I was born in Hartford, Connecticut, on September 22, 1942 and was named Dorothea Arlene Theresa Gagne. My mother, Rose Alma Belanger, named me after a close friend, Sister Dorothea. She was a nun with whom my mother had worked at St. Francis Hospital in Hartford. My mother was a nurse; I eventually followed her in that profession.

My mother said I was a war baby, because I was born during World War II. I was the fourth of five children. I look just like my father but take after my mother. Mom told me all about the times when she and Sister Dorothea worked hard during the wartime, staying prepared so as not to take any risk that the enemy would attack us in our country. There were civil defense tests once a month for the public. They would teach people how to do a proper blackout. You weren't allowed to have lights on after dark, just candles or flashlights. The shades we're pulled down, with the light color side on the inside, and dark colored side of the shade facing outdoors. It kept the light from shining through. In the event of an air raid, the enemy would not be able to see ground targets when they would try to sneak an attack under the cover of night.

I remember participating in drills at school. We had to hurry quietly; the nun's reminding us not run; down to the basement of the school to be safe in case of an attack. We never were afraid of the drills and understood what was required.

We had air raid shelters. These were places where people would go for safety. Most of them were in schools. A shelter would provide food, water, and protection much like our emergency shelters today. They had placards on the buildings so people knew just where to go.

The women knitted very fine cotton bandages for the injured soldiers who were serving overseas. My mother showed me the kind of cotton threads they used, and the needles were extremely tiny. They were a size 1, if I remember correctly. They also prepared packages for those who had gone to war. The servicemen and women would receive baked cookies, knitted socks, or a sweater as well as the bandages that were made with care. Sometimes a note would be added to let them know someone back home was thinking and praying for them. Women pulled together during the war and took over men's jobs. They worked in factories building parts to help the war effort. Whatever men did for jobs, women jumped right in to fill the gap and kept things going while they were called to fight for our country.

We owe the freedoms we have today to the men and women who served then and now.

Chapter 2

"Bring the whole tithe into the storehouse, that there may be food in my house. Test me in this and see that I will not throw open the flood gates of heaven and pour out so much blessing that you will not have room enough for it."

Malachi 3:10

God *always* takes care of those who share with the less fortunate. He cares for his own children who serve him. This means giving food and clothing to others, helping those in need, supporting our church, tithing, and so on. My mother understood this.

Times were tight. At six years of age, I saw how my mother always knew how to stretch a dollar. She had a generous spirit. Despite having little money, she always had a heart of gold. My mother would give the dress from her back if someone needed it. If people stopped by, she never failed to insist that they sit down and eat with us. She was good to everyone. She blessed many people in her life by being like a funnel for God, giving all she could to help others. Often, she would give things away.

We weren't wealthy, but we never lacked, because God used her as an instrument to help others and gave her an abundance of blessings in return. God blessed her for her kindness.

I see so much of my mother in myself—her personality and her giving heart. In my own life, I have followed in her footsteps by having the same giving heart. I'm very thankful for that. I get great pleasure in helping those who are in need in one way or another. More importantly, I feel good that I do what I do for God's glory. God always makes a way for me, even when I don't expect it. I am always amazed at all he does for me in my life. Have you ever met a generous person that is mean? No! Generous people are usually happy and confident, and they are very comfortable in their lives. It's not that they don't go through problems, but they have faith and also trust in God to get them through the tough stuff.

Chapter 3

My mother met my father at the hospital where she worked. Napoleon David Gagne was a patient of hers. He was in the hospital for a year because he had been in a serious motorcycle accident. His cousin had been killed in the same accident. My father was the first in Hartford Hospital to have a bone grafted from one leg into the other. After he was released from the hospital, he and my mother dated for a year. My dad was the youngest of sixteen siblings. He was raised on a dairy farm. He left home at the age of thirteen to live with his aunt in the United States.

My mom and dad were married on January 3, 1929.

Ma (which was what we called our mother) was a strong pillar in our home. We were raised to have faith in God, and we went to church every Sunday. When I think back, we always had evening prayers with my mother. We all had our own chair to kneel by to pray in our kitchen. She taught us that we must be willing to be funnels and share God's blessings with others in what we did for them.

Whatever my mother did was fine with my father. He enjoyed sitting back and watching her in whatever she was doing. He got a kick out of her! My father was a wonderful man; he was very quiet, the type of guy who minded his own business. I never heard him say a bad word about anyone. He was a hard worker. My father was very fair of complexion and had strawberry-blond hair in his younger years. He looked Irish or Swedish and had light-blue eyes, but he was French Canadian. People took me for Irish or Swedish too, based on my strawberry-red hair and hazel-green eyes. My father had a nickname for me in French, *Petite Blanche*, which means "little white one" or "little fair one," because of my coloring. My father was born in Weedon, Quebec, and spoke more French than English. He had a very heavy French Canadian accent.

My mother was born in New Bedford, Massachusetts. Her family was also French Canadian; my maternal grandparents were from Canada. French was the first language in our home as it had been for my mother growing up. Ma looked Italian with her olive complexion. My four siblings all looked like Mother. They had very dark brown hair and brown eyes.

My mother made everything from scratch. She baked a lot. If I pause and remember, I can still smell the delicious aroma of the baking bread in our kitchen. The bread was awesome! If I close my eyes, I can almost taste it now. She would cut us a slice while it was steaming hot and place a pat of butter on it. Yum, so delicious!

She always made great meals. Her roast pork, browned and crisp on top with a rich brown gravy for the mashed potatoes; homemade biscuits; and, for dessert, strawberry shortcake were all prepared for us after we got home from Sunday Mass. It was a wonderfully simple life. We always ate our meals together as a family.

Mom often worked double shifts at the hospital to help my father make ends meet. Dad made decent money but not enough for a family of seven. My mother worked in the operating room. She would also work on the units to get extra hours.

She helped my father any way she could, and they always worked as a team. They made sure we had what we needed. Ma knew how to stretch a dime; she handled all the finances in the home.

Things back then were not like today. People had no credit cards to get themselves into debt. There was no charging it then and paying for it later. Everything was paid with cash. You never went on vacation unless it was paid for. If a person didn't have the cash to go on a trip with his family, he made the best of it by staying home or doing small day trips.

My mother would often shop for us girls in secondhand stores. Back then, wealthy people donated clothes, so my mother bought us all beautiful taffeta dresses, velvet coats, scotch plaid pleated skirts (which I loved), and wool blazers. We wore leotards or knee socks to keep warm in the winter. They were priced at ten, twenty-five, or fifty cents—never more than a dollar.

I remember in the wintertime we used an old-fashioned cast-iron cook stove that had a large kerosene bottle hooked to the back of it. It had a bin that was used to heat water for our bath in addition to being used for cooking. It also had an oven with a chrome footrest and a pie and bread warmer on the top. The footrest was great. We would come in from outdoors with our feet cold and place our feet on the chrome footrest to warm our toes with the oven door open. For our snack, mom would fix us Ovaltine or malted milk.

My father had to walk to the corner gas station to get the kerosene for the cook stove. I remember being only four years old and going to the gas station in a snowstorm. My father pulled me on the sled and hauled a kerosene bottle on it as well. I was my father's pet, because I looked just like him. I was bundled up in my snowsuit and rubber boots. I was thrilled to go out with him and to be in the snow. We also stopped off at the local pharmacy and picked up my mother's medication. While we were there, George, the owner and pharmacist of the pharmacy, sat me up on the tall stool while he filled my mother's medication for asthma. He always gave me a vanilla cream soda and called me Tootsie. It was the nickname he gave me. Then off we went, my father pulling me on the sled through the blizzard back home, which was only a couple blocks away. I'm so happy I was raised in that era. All my memories of the 1940s are wonderful.

Chapter 4

Our Christmases were the old-fashioned sort. We celebrated them the simple way, remembering that this was the season of the birth of our Savior, Jesus Christ. We went to church every Christmas Eve at midnight.

A beautiful manger was set up with the Christ child, Mary, and Joseph. It was surrounded with fragrant pine branches, and the aroma was so inviting it seemed to fit the scene.

I loved those years, because it was a simple and pure time, not like today with all the hype of the holidays and the barrage of commercials urging us to spend a ton of money on material things, with Jesus forgotten by most.

Our tree was set up on Christmas Eve. The aroma of the pine tree was welcoming and festive. We decorated it with large, multicolored lights and strung popcorn and cranberries with dried orange slices. Under the tree was a manger. It also had pine branches with their lovely aroma just like the one at church. Mother would read us stories about the nativity.

She also read "'Twas the Night Before Christmas" and other Christmas stories. We received two gifts each, which was the custom back then in the fifties. Candy canes and fruit, such as oranges and apples, were common to have in our stockings. Everyone would get so excited to find a book of Life Savers in our stockings as well, because they were only sold as a book with all the different rolls of flavors at Christmas time. Since there were five children, my mother would make us homemade candy, fudge, and cookies.

Ma always had fruitcake she bought with lots of nuts and fruit. It was our traditional Christmastime treat.

That's the way families celebrated Christmas then.

My childhood was a wonderful one.

I never remember missing church growing up and always attended the high holidays, Christmas and Easter. They were very important. At Christmas, we were taught about the birth of Jesus. Leading up to Easter, we fasted and gave up something we loved for lent as our own sacrifice for Jesus and what He did for us on the cross. On Good Friday, we had a moment of silence in our home to remember the time of Jesus's death on the cross.

He gave himself as a young man of thirty-three years to the cross for our sins. He made Himself a living sacrifice, because He loved us so much.

We were raised knowing right and wrong and having godly values and morals. We were to treat others the way we would want to be treated and were not to laugh at those underprivileged or handicapped.

We never saw ourselves as poor as others might have thought. We ate well, were dressed well, and were well loved.

I attended private schools taught by the French sisters of the Holy Spirit. My mother's two sisters were of the same order, so we could attend private French schools free of charge. During the afternoon, speaking French in class was mandatory; we had to whether we could or not, and we learned the hard way. We also spoke French in our home.

I wanted to be a servant of God from childhood. I always had an interest in serving God and had a hunger for Him and His Word. As the years went by and I grew up, I read a lot about the saints and martyrs that sacrificed their lives to serve the Lord Jesus Christ. I found it very interesting to read how the martyrs went to the stakes and gave up their lives for their faith in Christ. Could I be so faithful to love the Lord so much?

Little did I know what God had in store for me later in my life.

Chapter 5

At twenty-one years of age, I decided to go study to be a nurse. I graduated from Hartford Hospital Nursing School in 1962. I worked hard and was so proud of my navy-blue cape with gold trim and white nurse's uniform with its white cap, white stockings, and shoes. That was when nurses looked like nurses. Now it's scrubs. I graduated from the same place my mother had received her nurse's training.

I remember the day when Ma put my nurse's cap on me for the first time. I knew that I was following her vocation and path of generosity for my life. It was one of the proudest moments for me and probably for her as well. The memory still brings tears of joy to my eyes.

When I started dating, I always dated military men. I guess the reason for that was that we lived near the Navy submarine base an hour away. Several of our family served in the military, and there was never a time when we didn't have someone from the base over. They all were friends of my older sister Alice. Many sailors stayed friends with my mother and father after my sister married. They continued to come to our home to see my parents. Mom always made them feel at home, and there was always enough food for them. She would have sailors over for Sunday dinner, since they were far away from their own homes. The sailors adopted my parents like their own. They called my mother Mom.

My mother and father loved the military. My family was always patriotic. Even after the sailors got out of the service, they would call my mother to see how the family was doing.

I had many nice dates, and the sailors always respected me. I knew God intended intimacy between a man and a woman to be sacred, and I wanted to stay celibate for when I got married.

I met Gustav Woodrum in 1957. He was in the Navy attending submarine school in Groton Ct. after being transferred from San Diego, California. The same day Gustav turned eighteen, he entered the Navy for basic training.

From the time we met, he always told me he wanted to be married to me, have children, and settle down. I didn't believe it; how could he know that when he hardly knew me? I knew I wasn't ready for marriage and still wanted to date. I was too young to think of marriage. I had decided I wanted a good man who would to go to church with me and be with me the rest of my life. After two years of dating, I found I was always comparing the other men I dated to Gus. I liked the way he treated my parents and how he loved them. He always told them he considered them more his parents then his own. In his childhood, his father hadn't been a good father, and his mother never had stood up to him, so the children went without food and clothing. Gustav and my brother Raymond were close. He won my parents over. He had a good heart and was a very good man.

In time, after dating a while, I knew he would make a good family man and also a good husband and provider. He was very sincere in all he did.

He was gone on a submarine run to Ireland and England for three months for sea trials. They called it Spring Board. I found I was missing him. He always had told my parents he would get me down the aisle no matter what. He would end up with me. I got angry with that, but deep down I knew I would end up with him. He chased me long enough. When he came home to my parents' house, he said he couldn't wait much more for me. He wanted to marry me, and for the last time he proposed to me again, I said yes.

I spoke to my parents about it and asked if they would approve. I was Catholic, and he was from a Methodist background even though he and his family didn't attend. They gave me the okay to marry him. My mother said, "There is only one God and no religion in heaven. It's not religion that gets us to heaven; it's our faith and accepting Jesus in our hearts and serving him." My mother went with us downtown to the jeweler. Gustav wanted her to come with us to pick out my diamond, and it was beautiful. It just so happened that already engraved on the inside of the ring were the words, "Together Forever." What a sign from God that was! God had his hand in my life and Gus's.

We married on July 2, 1960, two weeks before he was to go to the Philadelphia naval shipyard to dry-dock for boat repairs for six months.

It was the best thing that ever happened to us. He was simply crazy about me and vice versa. He called me his angel.

I only wish now I would have kept all my letters and his from when he was in the Navy, but when you're young, you don't think about such things. We loved each other, and it was hard having him go to sea. Military life involves a lot of sacrificing. He was on fast-attack submarines that went out for long periods of time. We were in Philadelphia for six months, and then we were stationed at the submarine base in Groton, Connecticut. I remained in Hartford for the time being.

Chapter 6

On October 21, 1961, I gave birth to our daughter, Rose Alma. She was a beautiful baby girl that weighed in at eight pounds, nine ounces. She was twenty-three-and-a-half inches long. Born at 11:00 p.m., she had jet-black hair, blue eyes, and rosy cheeks like Snow White.

Gus was over in the Mediterranean in the Azores, submerged several feet below the sea. He came home three months after she was born and saw her for the first time.

After she was born and about two years old, we got stationed in Bainbridge, Maryland, so Gus could go to gyro school to learn how to maneuver a ship or submarine at sea. He also attended Navy recruiting school to be trained to recruit men and women into the armed forces. He was a very brilliant man, and I was very proud of him. He was quite handsome in his Navy blues with the gold buttons and officer's hat.

I then became pregnant with my son, Paul Glenn.

It was a terrible summer in Maryland. The heat and the fleas and ticks were almost unbearable. I wasn't used to that, having lived only in New England. I hated it. While in the military,

Gustav always placed his family first as much as possible. He was never a man to go drink with the guys the way most did. As an officer, he was a real example of how men should conduct themselves.

He always seemed to have connections somewhere. We then got transferred to Plainville, Connecticut, and the years that followed were the happiest of our life. Gus was home every night while on recruiting duty there for four years.

Paul was born August 31, 1964, at 12:55 p.m. weighing in at seven pounds, ten ounces and twenty-one-and-a-half inches long, he was a beautiful baby boy. He was adorable. He was born with bright red hair and green eyes and rosy cheeks. I guess most babies are born with rosy cheeks. He was the best baby any mother could want. He slept all night even when he was teething! As an infant, Rose Alma had a heart murmur and needed extra attention. Sometimes she was up crying all night, needing to be rocked. She soon learned, though, that she would be rocked anytime she cried. Babies are very smart and learn right off how to get their way.

We were transferred to Groton Submarine Base after four years on recruiting duty. It was very hard to move from Plainville. It was great living in our small military community with other Army, Navy, and Marine families. The wives lived there while the men served in Vietnam along with families whose husbands were recruiters like my husband. My sister Lorraine lived only three houses down from us. We did almost everything together—sewing, knitting, and taking long walks with the kids. She had two boys. Her husband came home on the weekends from Brooklyn, New York, where his ship was.

He was stationed there for three years. All week, my sister and I did a lot together. I even helped her learn how to drive. My sister always said those were the best years of her life as well. I cried when we had to leave. I still remember going for sled rides in the snowstorms as Gus pulled us along behind the Navy recruiter's car in his uniform when he got home. He was in charge of five recruiting offices: NYC Times Square; Plainville, CT; New Britain, CT; New Rochelle, NY; and White Plains NY. He always made quota and supplied all the other stations with new recruits. He was even chosen as Navy recruiter of the year. Gus didn't like having to go back to sea again.

Few people know what a military wife goes through to keep the home going and to raise the children mostly by herself. She is a hero in her own right. It was sometimes a lonely life. I hated Gustav being away so much. I missed him. But I knew we both had a responsibility—mine to keep things going on the home front, and his to do his duty at sea.

My mother would say, "A woman who is married to a military man is married to his sea bag as well. You are part of the U.S. government now; they own you."

Chapter 7

I met Amy in 1968 in Mystic, Connecticut, at the nursing home we worked in. It was small, with only fourteen patients, and it had a family atmosphere. I was always curious about the Bible and wanted answers, so when I was going to work with her for the first time one evening, a nurse on days who was giving me report said to me, "You're going to be working with a real fanatic, a Jesus nut."

I replied to her, "Good!" That was just the kind of person I wanted to meet. She might have answers for me about the Bible. She had been a Christian all her life. She answered all the questions I asked her. I was very impressed with her, and she was very interesting. Amy was persistent with me; I was a real challenge for her. She told me after I got saved and gave my heart to Christ that God gave her a revelation that I was going to be the one to win souls with her. She had been praying that God would send her someone to help her in that area. I was that someone!

She taught me all about salvation and how to get saved. I was always calling her on the phone, asking her about different scriptures I didn't understand. She was patient with me and had the wisdom and the patience of Job. She taught me how important scripture is for us to draw close to God. She gave me a Bible, and I was anxious to learn. I got saved during a revival they were having at her church, and I attended with her and another nurse who worked with us. It was totally different from what I had experienced in the Catholic Church.

At first, I wasn't interested in going all the time, and sometimes I went just so she would stop pestering me. She was always after me to attend. On one particular Sunday, the congregation was singing and clapping their hands. I leaned over and asked her, "Why are they clapping and raising their hands?"

She responded to me, "Now, Dottie, if you were at a ball game and your favorite team was winning, wouldn't you be excited, cheering and clapping?"

"Yes," I replied.

She said, "Well, we're on God's side, and we know we are going to win at the end. So we have reason to shout and clap when singing about Jesus!"

What a great illustration that was! She was always doing that and always had an answer. It all made sense. So I started attending church there, at the Church of God in Groton. I didn't know then, but God did, that I would need the people in the church for prayer.

Chapter 8

One Friday evening when my husband was out to sea, I was doing some cleaning in the house when I had an urge to go with my children to visit my parents, who lived an hour away in Hartford. I left the mop in the pail and furniture polish on the table and said to the kids, "Let's go for a ride and see Pepere and Memere." (That's French for Grandmother and Grandfather.)

I was lonesome with my husband being away and wanted to get out for a while with the kids. Weekends were always the hardest.

While there at my parents, we were getting ready to play Parcheesi and the kids were coloring in their coloring books when we heard an ambulance go by.

I said to my mother, "My God, it must be a serious accident—they're really flying by here." That was about 6:00 p.m. We continued to play our game and then got the kids settled in for bed, since my parents said we should just spend the night. We didn't know the ambulance we had heard was the first sign of the news that was yet to come.

My brother had been shot five times with a .38-caliber pistol at close range.

It was 9:00 p.m. My father had headed off to bed, and my mother and I had just sat down with hot chocolate when the phone rang.

My father answered the phone, and he didn't understand what they were telling him. He misunderstood, and instead of giving my mother the phone, he told my mother that my brother Raymond had been seriously injured. He was in the hospital. My dad assumed it was Raymond, because he was supposed to come in that night from Norfolk, Virginia. He was in the Navy, and back then many sailors used to hitchhike to get home. It wasn't Raymond. It was my brother Wilfred (we called him Sonny), who lived down the road from my parents. He had been shot with a .38 at close range and was in the hospital and was in surgery as we spoke. My brother had eighteen pints of blood on arrival to the ER.

His chest and stomach were like a strainer. As fast as the blood went in, the blood came right out. His heart stopped five times on his way up to surgery. After twelve hours, the surgeon came down for a moment to tell us if he survived he would be a vegetable. They said it was because he had fragments of bullets in him, including one bullet imbedded in his spine. The main artery that supplied the oxygen to the brain had been shattered, so he would be left a vegetable.

My mother and I understood the medical aspects. I was glad that I had become close to the Lord and had been saved. I had never expected something like this to take place with my brother, but God had prepared me. I could never have handled it the way I did if I hadn't been close to the Lord. I felt a hand on my shoulder and heard His voice tell me very clearly, "Your brother is going to live." When all was so bleak and all odds were against him, God spoke as clear as a bell to me. I will never forget that. He was my fortress at this time of my life.

I was now the strong pillar in the family, walking in my mother's footsteps, when this happened.

My husband was gone for four months, and there was no way to get him home. When the submarine was out on a top-secret mission, patrols stayed submerged and did not surface.

After three weeks in the ICU with steady critical care, Sonny saw Jesus by his bed and spoke to him. At this point, he didn't even know who we were. Once again, it was proof to me that Jesus was alive and truly showed me how much God loved my brother. You see, my brother never had believed in Jesus and the cross. He used to mock the cross in my mother's home, and we would just shudder at his terrible remarks. He would say to us that he would just as soon have spit on the cross.

There in his hospital bed, he held long conversations with Jesus. It was all in a whispered tone of voice, and he always had a gentle smile on his face.

After several weeks, when Sonny came around, he described Jesus to us. My brother became a believer after that, because he saw Jesus face-to-face. He said Jesus spoke with him all the time and said how much He loved him.

Sonny never had any damage to his brain. He walked and never needed a wheelchair or to live in a nursing home as the doctors had predicted. It was truly a miracle.

Chapter 9

God knew what was in store for me when Gus retired from the Navy. He was ahead of me—His Holy Spirit building me up, preparing me, and giving me strength for all the challenges that were ahead for us.

It was 1974 when we bought land in northeast Vermont. We thought it would be a good place to finish raising our children. God allowed us to buy forty-seven acres at a hundred dollars an acre, which was unthought-of then, when land now goes for twelve hundred to fifteen hundred dollars an acre. Our home was built on top of a high hill looking over the lake and the country town road. It was a beautiful view.

Transitioning to civilian life certainly involved culture shock after living a military life. Wow, what a difference! It was a tough adjustment for me most of all. There were heavy snowstorms and bitterly cold weather. The first spring there, the snow came up to my waist!

With military life and church life, there is community, and being out here in Vermont away from what I knew, I felt isolated and lonely. Vermont then had more cows than people. My friends called it the lost nation. Gus had his health issues, and my daughter Rose suffered a bad concussion when she struck her head on a beam while helping her father. I missed my church family and friends. I felt awful. I knew I needed to lean harder on God, and I did. There is a comforting feeling that comes from knowing when we feel lonely we are not alone. It seemed that every time I got sad and homesick for my friend Amy and her husband Jack, the phone rang, and it was her! She gave me encouragement and prayed for me. It seems the Holy Spirit quickened her heart so that she knew to call me just when I needed it most. Jack and Amy drove up to see us every three weeks or so. I was ever so happy to have them show up and stay for a few days. Jack and Gus were very close, and we had a great time fellowshipping with one another. Amy would play the guitar, and we would sing hymns. Many times, their kids came up as well. What a wonderful time it was!

God is good, and when you're in His plan, He will do anything to show you what He wants done in your life. He spoke to my heart and told me my house was going to be a lighthouse to the lost and I would see many saved. It turned out to be true. God had a work for me, and He started speaking to me through His Holy Spirit—guiding me, showing me, and giving me a vision and purpose.

I started meeting people and sharing God's word with them. The first person was a neighbor who ended up being my first friend in Vermont. She gave her heart to the Lord.

I applied for a job at the Medical Center Hospital of Vermont in Burlington. I was hired and placed on the neurosurgical floor.

The brain is the most mysterious part of the body and very unpredictable. I was placed on rotating shifts, which was mandatory, and loved the challenge. I did this for quite a while before I joined the visiting nurses, which was my true passion. I loved going to visit homes and giving nursing care. It was so much more personal. I would see six to seven patients in a day. It gave me an opportunity to share God's love with the clients.

It was something I decided I was called to do after my husband died of cancer in 1984. That is how I got into hospice after being with VNA for ten years.

✝

Chapter 10

May 11, 1976. It was 9:00 a.m. when the phone rang. It was the weekend, and I had just finished my breakfast. I answered it, and when I heard my mother's voice I knew something wasn't right. My father had had a massive heart attack and died in his sleep. She had overslept, which was unusual for her. She had gotten up to cook my father some breakfast. When she had returned, she had been unable to wake him and had realized he was gone. My mom was in shock. We all were. My dad had a large funeral in Harford.

I sang "Golden Street Parade" to myself to remind myself that I would see my dad again one day.

My husband died of colon cancer at forty-eight-years–old, two weeks after his birthday. He had been sick for two years. I had just turned forty-two.

This time in my life was very difficult for me. It challenged everything I knew as a nurse, because Gus was not just a patient. He was the love of my life. Not only was he struggling with the colon cancer, but he would later be diagnosed with brain cancer. Every day came with challenges, struggles, and tears. Gus always had a positive outlook and was always humorous. He was in the hospital in serious condition, and the doctors had prepared the family that his time was coming to a close. I was exhausted from staying long hours with Gus at the hospital and didn't want to leave for fear he would pass while I was home freshening up. The nurse told me I needed to rest, and they would contact me if Gus's condition changed. Reluctantly, I went home. As I was getting ready to head back to the hospital, the phone rang. I picked up the phone, and to my amazement, it was Gus! He said, "Hi, honey!"

I was shocked. I said "Gus? What are you doing?"

He replied, "I didn't know if I was checking in or checking out! I'm sitting on the end of the bed having cookies and milk. Come on up!" That was Gus.

The two things that were constant were God's love for us and our love for each other. It was hard to watch him slowly slipping away from this world. I asked one day, "Gus, are you ever angry at God?"

He said to me, "Come here and let's talk. If God is done with me, then I will go be with him. Until then, I don't question God and what I have, so don't you."

I told him I didn't, but it is hard to see other couples growing old together when we will never be able to.

When Gus set his mind to something, he saw it through. Sickness did not stop him. One thing he wanted to do before he wasn't able to was drive down to Connecticut and see Jack and Amy one more time. It took twelve hours to make what was usually a five-hour trip, but he did it. He spent the week doing what was most important to him—spending time with the ones he loved.

When Amy and Jack brought him back, they stayed, and I remember one night while we were singing and worshiping as we had done in the past, despite the cancer in his body that was taking its toll, Gus raised his hands. I thought he was reaching up with his long arms to hold my hand, but he was actually raising them to hold his loving Savior's. Nothing would come between him and his Lord.

We picked out our cemetery plots the week before he died. Gus went to be with our Lord two weeks before Christmas. My daughter, Rose, mentioned, "Dad always loved hearing you sing," and so I did. He passed from this life to the next while I sang to him softly in his ear "Where the Roses Never Fade" and "The Eastern Gate" as the family stood around his bedside.

The priest, who was a friend of ours, said how Gustav had taught us how to live and to die at his funeral service. With all the pain he was going through, he never complained. He was always positive. His faith grew strong through his sickness. He never wavered in his faith and placed his life into God's hands. I had a wonderfully blessed life with Gus.

Chapter 11

It wasn't more than four years later when I was once more faced with the loss of a person I loved with all my heart, the one by whose example I tried to pattern my life, my pillar, my encourager, my Ma.

A man who had Alzheimer's and wasn't supposed to be behind the wheel stole the keys to a car and drove away without his family knowing it. He drove through a stop sign and hit my daughter's car broadside, and the car was thrown into a pasture across the highway. The Jaws of Life had to remove my mother from the car. My daughter was injured. She had glass imbedded in her face around her mouth and in her scalp. Her left arm was injured. My nephew was in the backseat but wasn't injured; he was just an infant safe in a car seat. My mother received the brunt of the impact, because the car hit the passenger's side. She was in the hospital three and a half weeks with multiple injuries. She knew in her heart she was going to die and spoke to me about it.

She was discharged on Holy Thursday of Easter week. I noticed that her knee was black and blue, and as a nurse, I was concerned that it heralded a possible blood clot, so I asked her if the nurse knew. Mom said yes; however, she hadn't mentioned anything about the knee to the nurse. My daughter, Rose Alma (named after my mother), had gone to the pharmacy to get Mother's pain medication to fill the prescription for what she needed at home. VNA was coming in to start her physical therapy the next morning on Good Friday at 10:00 a.m.

Mom had a restless night, and I was up with her several times. She just didn't seem to get comfortable. She told me in French that she hoped to get better—she didn't want to burden us—and mentioned a nursing home. I said, "No way! You are staying with us." I knew she was feeling bad from the pain of a fractured pelvis. She still had a long road of recovery before her with physical therapy.

The next morning, Ma was in the kitchen eating some breakfast when she laid her head down on the table and said, "Do you think I'm going to make it, Dottie?"

I said, "Yes, Ma, you just feel bad because you've suffered a lot of injuries; it's going to take time."

"Do you really think so?" she asked.

It was 9:00 a.m. Ma wanted to lie down in her bedroom until the visiting nurses were supposed to arrive, and she asked Danielle, her great-granddaughter, to get her mother to help her to the bathroom. My daughter, Rose, helped my mother to the commode. When Ma was finished, she said to Rose, "Now put me to bed. I'm going to die." Rose helped her up. As she stood Ma up to pivot her to the bed, she asked my mother, "Memere, help me and stand so I won't drop you." That's when my mother's head dropped back. She passed away in my daughter's arms. She died on Good Friday on my father's birthday.

It was a blood clot that lodged in her lung. We were in shock, but I had been able to see that my mother was making preparations to leave here and see her Savior. With the loss of Ma, I felt empty. We all did. My daughter blamed herself for the accident. She said, "If only we had stopped for hot chocolate as Memere wanted to, she would be alive." I told her it wasn't her fault; that's why it's called an accident.

God spoke to my heart and reminded me often that she went the way she wanted to go. She never wanted to die alone. She died with us at home. Ma loved the Lord and was ready to be with her loved ones, Jesus, and my father. The Bible says to be absent from the body is to be present with the Lord. She believed it.

Oh how I miss my parents and Gus, but I know that I have that blessed assurance that we will meet again someday in heaven, where the sting of death will be no more. We will reunite and walk the streets of gold together once more. Amen!

Chapter 12

I had been working for about five years when a colleague approached me and asked to speak to me. I really liked her and had a lot of respect for her. She told me she was starting up a hospice team in VNA. She asked me to join her new team. I was excited and accepted the offer. I still continued doing home care visits on my own team when the hospice work was slow.

I worked with paraplegics and quads as well, which helped out the teams when I had down time. The patients were usually mad at the world and could be difficult because of the state of dependency they were in. It was understandable. One minute you're independent, doing your own thing, and the next, your private space has been stripped away and you are totally dependent on others.

Hospice work became my new passion as well as the home-care visits.

There was such a sense of fulfillment in serving end-stage patients. They appreciated their nurses and the care and help we gave them and their families. We were there to help patients through their anxieties and fears about what they were going through, facing mortality and what lay ahead.

The families were overwhelmed with how to care for those they loved that were dying. They struggled with the same thoughts and worries their loved ones did. That was when I came in and shared my thoughts and experiences to reassure them and bring comfort and support as well as teaching them how to care for their loved ones. They hired us so we could take over to help the family and patient.

My job was also to ease into patient caretaking when the family was unable to so they no longer had the stress and weight of around-the-clock care. When it came to their spiritual care, I always had to be led by the Spirit before I shared with them. God is always on time; He is never late. People think hospice is only caring about physical and emotional needs, but it involves taking care of spiritual needs as well. Each of us was created with a body, a soul, and a spirit. No matter how rich or poor a person is, when it's all said and done, a person in his or her last stages of life is ready to hear God's Word and the message of His love, because he or she desperately wants to be sure things are right with God before slipping into eternity.

There have been a select few that have made a big impression on my life. They all come from different walks of life, and that's what makes my work for God special. Since I retired from working with the VNA hospice, I still find myself having a strong, burning desire to care for end-stage patients. Today, I provide hospice care privately, and I like it that way. I get many referrals, and when I am needed, the people who call know my work is more than just hospice; it's also my ministry, and they know whom I represent—my Lord, Jesus Christ.

Because of all I have been through, I can share all the experiences in my life, and patients and family members know I can sympathize with what they are going through. In my hospice work, I can honestly share how God has used me, and they know it's genuine and comes from the heart.

Three years ago, I was diagnosed with DCIS (ductal carcinoma in situ)—cancer of the milk ducts. Because of that, I had to have a partial mastectomy. I totally believed in God's help, so I told the surgeon that I had a master physician and he would be his eyes and guide his hands. I am not ashamed to share God and what He does for me. The Doctor could not believe how fast I recovered and said it was because of my great attitude. I knew better. We know it's God that does it all when we put our trust in Him. He had shown Himself faithful previously in my life when I found out I had early-stage cervical cancer. God took care of me then as well. I thank God for all his goodness. I have been tested and tried and still have my finish line; when I go to heaven, it will be worth it all.

"Even though I walk through the shadow of death, I will fear no evil, for your rod and your staff, they comfort me" (Psalm 23:4).

When my patients become fearful of the unknown, I reassure them with this Psalm. I have had many trials and tests, and God has used them to teach me and build my character. I know God is with me; His presence and guidance provide comfort. He has done so much in my life and has seen me through it all. I have received the gifts of the Holy Spirit. Acts 2:43 says, "Everyone was filled with awe, and many wonders and miraculous signs were done by the apostles." The apostles performed many miracles, casting out demons, speaking in tongues, and healing the sick. If we just give our Abba, our Father, a chance, He will prove himself to us. He knew us before we were knit together in our mothers' wombs and called us by name. How much more, then, can God do for us if we are faithful and put our trust in Him?

In the continuing pages of this book are stories about some of my different relationships and blessed encounters with those patients who impacted my life and still do today.

Chapter 13

Mrs. T lived in a beautiful section of Vermont who had cancer in her eye. It also had metastasized to her brain. She was the type person who always had a positive attitude and she never talked about her sickness. She focused on her husband, her son and the time she had left.

She developed the cancer from an accident at her son's little league baseball game. The ball was hit, and came into the stands striking her in the eye. Over time she developed eye cancer. She was only thirty eight years of age and her son was ten.

One of the things that clinics and hospice do is to help children understand what a parent with cancer is going through by using visual therapy. They would ask the kids to draw what they understood about the illness. Mrs. T son would draw his mother with a big black eye and the word "Splat!"

She had suffered for about four months before they found that her treatments weren't working and making her sicker. She had developed painful sores in her mouth from thrush and was not able to eat.

My job was to get Mrs. T. ready for her chemo appointments.

I would help her with her bathing, and lay out her clothes she wanted to wear that day. Due to the treatments she was receiving, she would always feel cold so she loved velour jogging suits. They were so warm and soft. She grew up in the era that a women wasn't completely dressed until she had her make up on. She would apply bright red lipstick which symbolized for her bravery, and made sure she wore her favorite cologne which smelled like gardenias. Mrs. T would then put on her pink bandana to cover her head from where her hair had fallen out from the radiation & chemo treatments. I would apply a fresh sterile dressing to her eye and she would finish off the whole ensemble with a pair of stunning earrings.

Mrs. T was a wonderful mother to her son and her husband was always by her side.

She would enjoy it when her son and I would bake warm, gooey, oatmeal raisin cookies, fresh out of the oven. The smell of the cookies baking would fill the house and make her mouth water.

She went through a time of depression which was common for people going through this. We had a connection because she knew that I had been through some of the same things with my husband Gus's sickness.

She said there was something different about me than the other nurses. I told her it was the love of Christ. I told her about a song I liked. The chorus had a line in it that said, "He washed my eyes with tears..." The song was about life's trials and how He suffered and died for us and for our sins, and thru His tears He wiped away our tears.

She came to accept the gift of eternal life and had such a peace about the things ahead. She knew that God was in control and would watch over her son and husband.

As time was getting short for her to live, she would have her son climb up on the bed to "snuggle" next to her and tell him stories of where she would go when she leaves. She told him she was going to a special garden where only mother's would be allowed to go and she wouldn't be sick anymore. It was a special garden where fairies lived and at twilight time and they would fly around in the garden with stars twinkling and the moon beams reflecting off the water. She would have her son mesmerized in what it would be like. She didn't want her son to worry and she wanted him to know God would take good care of her.

"Momma, do you have to go away like you tell me? Why do you need to go away? I love you and want you to stay with daddy and me."

I won't have to be sick anymore. Plus, I can get the beautiful new home God gives us, ready for us all to live in someday. In the mean time you will need to help daddy be strong. She told him that Jesus was short of help, and she wanted to go help Him and His angels. He thought that his mom was an angel.

One day I noticed that she was sitting in her recliner, gazing out the window, lost in thought. There was a bird feeder right outside the window where she could watch the chickadees and cardinals feed and play.

I asked her what she was thinking about. She said she was

concerned for her husband and son when she was gone. She hoped that her son would remember her.

I told her that God has a way of bringing the ones we love to our minds.

Mrs. T passed away just before Easter.

Years went by, and her son was twenty three when he came to visit us at our Hospice Conference and gave his testimony. He spoke about all of the things his "Beautiful Mother" had taught him.

He presently gives speeches in honor of his mother at conferences to help others who have suffered the loss of parent or loved one.

Each year on the date of her death he releases a bouquet of white & pink balloons into the sky with his dad in her memory.

Mrs. T got her wish. Her son would always remember her.

Chapter 14

Mr. H's family didn't have any inkling of how to care for him or what to do. They were in desperate need of help and were thrilled to see our Christian hospice group come in. It's simply amazing how people are. The first thing out of the daughter's mouth was that she and her father were not believers. They felt that Jesus was just a nice man who had done nice things, but they didn't really believe that He was the Son of God come in the flesh. Mr. H was an atheist; so was his daughter. This made things very interesting, since they had hired a Christian hospice group. They had called hospice and asked for "Caring Christian Women." It's a nonprofit that my best friend Amy started.

When I walked into Mr. H's room upstairs to meet him, he was very sweet and greeted me with a big smile. He had big bright eyes and a gentle way about him. He was only able to speak in a whisper, because he was very weak.

Mr. H had had a very successful life. His carton-making business included among its clients L'Oreal, Noxzema, Avon, and many other companies. His company designed the covers of the boxes and then boxed the products up for the companies.

They were another influential family that had a beautiful home a block from the ocean. It sat so it had a lovely view of the ocean from their bedrooms, and the guest room had a view of a lighthouse as well.

The master bedroom, where Mr. H was bedridden, had a huge fireplace, which was still used in the cold months. Outside, they had a beautiful trellis with ivy growing on it and landscaped gardens around the surrounding area. They had it all.

Mr. and Mrs. H had met at a debutante ball. Mr. H had told his buddy that he was there to dance with the most beautiful girl at the ball, and he did and then later married her. They raised five children, and he also served in the U.S. Army as an officer under General Eisenhower, who was his boss in France during the war. When Eisenhower got out, he took Mr. H with him to Washington to be his assistant there. I saw the big, signed picture of General Eisenhower hanging on his wall.

Mrs. H was a Christian and did a lot of charity work. She showed extraordinary patience when her husband and daughter made their remarks about God, since they did not believe. She was very easy going and let the things they said just slide.

Mr. and Mrs. H were very close and deeply in love still after fifty-five or more years. Mrs. H told me that Mr. H was proud that she, at sixty-five years of age, had gone back to school to get her master's degree in art history. He had taken her on a trip to Egypt as a gift to mark the accomplishment.

On Thanksgiving Day, he took a tumble on his daughter's tennis court. He was eighty-four years old, very active, and a pro at tennis. No one could match him. He always won. He was that good. He was physically fit at his age. He had just purchased a new Mercedes through a special order, and it sure was a beauty. He drove by himself to upstate New York for his meetings to take care of business.

After his fall, he didn't feel very well. It wasn't till after his death that the family found out he kept a small journal in his pocket where he wrote about his pain each day, how he was feeling, and how he was dealing with it.

When he returned to New London, he was in a lot of pain and couldn't hide it any longer. When he came back from his business trip, he went to see a friend, a tennis partner, who was also a doctor. That's when things quickly took a turn for the worse. He had lost the feeling in his legs from the waist down.

He was taken to Spartan Hospital in Boston, where they specialize in strokes and rehab paraplegics etc. He was there from after Thanksgiving into December. Because he was bedridden, he developed a bedsore at the tailbone and it became ulcerated. It had to be treated and changed with sterile dressings each day. My heart went out to him and the family—especially to him, since he was the one with this terrible situation. They kept the severity of it from him. He didn't even realize he wasn't able to walk anymore. They took test after test and found nothing. They never found what was wrong, and their solution was to send him home to die.

The H's were very special to me. Mr. H and I became very close in the short time I was there—two months, to be exact. I came to him on January 3, and he died February 12.

Our short time together was one I will cherish. When I would walk in at 8:00 a.m., he would be all wide eyes and smiles and say, "Hello my sparkle girl!" He loved my eyes and said they sparkled when I spoke. I would reply, "Top of the morning to you!" I would walk over and give him a good-morning kiss on his cheek. His wife called me their Manna from heaven. I wish I could have known him and Mrs. H when he wasn't sick. With my line of work and ministry, I meet people when they're at the end of their lives from a terminal illness. In the morning, when I would come in, I would shave him and prepare his very tiny breakfast of applesauce, oatmeal, pudding, and a glass of juice. Then he would be very tired and would have to rest awhile.

Now and then, the daughter would remind me, "You know, Dad and I are not believers." My response to her was always the same: "That's okay. We all have our own thoughts and beliefs one way or another, but I know my God is real, and He will help your father." She would reply, "I hope so." She told me her father was scared to die and had been en route to Spartan Hospital in Boston from New London Hospital when he had seen a black hole. It had frightened him.

On another trip to Boston, again, on the way home, he saw a black tunnel, which was deep. It put tremendous fear in him. He had so much fear that he often asked his daughter, "I won't have to go into that black tunnel again, will I?" That was a big concern for him. Sometimes he was afraid to fall asleep for fear of going into the black tunnel.

Chapter 15

After I started working there, he always had great expectations of my coming in to care for him. He was so fearful of dying. Again, another person of wealth never was giving God a second thought. His money was his god. But when it comes down to the nitty-gritty and all is said and done, they are willing to listen in their last days or weeks. Because they are going to die and realize their money won't save their eternal souls, they become very interested in knowing about eternity and God. They develop a different attitude and are receptive to learning about salvation then.

He was a man that had lived a privileged life. In the short time I had with him, I could see how he would be a popular and well-liked person with everyone that knew him. His wife was the same. I called them Mr. and Mrs. Wonderful. I really enjoyed them. She called Mr. H her silver fox. How cute.

I am at ease with people who are in their final days, and I'm not afraid to talk to them and comfort them. The Holy Spirit guides me when determining what to say to them. I always have words to reassure them that there is nothing to be fearful of, because Jesus is right there with them. I tell them I am not fearful of death because I know one's spirit continues to live. Most patients are fearful of the unknown.

I have explained, "When we die, our spirits, not our bodies, continue on. We leave the bodies we have now, which are temporary, to have our spirits continue onto our eternal home. God's word says in 2 Corinthians 5:8–9 that to be absent from the body is to be present with the Lord. Won't that be wonderful?" They agree with me, and then they have a peace.

We are living in the last days, and we need to throw out a lifeline to the lost. "The harvest is wide; the workers are few." (Matthew 9:37-38)

We must labor while there is still time. My job is to win souls that are in their final days or months of life. I always ask them if they know where they're going after they leave here. Some people don't know or haven't given it any thought. As I stated, Mr. H was one of those people.

I was surfing the channels in his room, trying to find something for us to watch. I thought I wouldn't turn to a Christian channel, because I knew his beliefs and didn't want to impose on him.

I was skipping past the 700 Club when and he told me, "Stop! I want to watch that channel." I had already been sharing God's love with him through my actions, and it must have been softening his heart. I was different from anyone he knew. The two incidents he experienced with the black tunnel that went deep still haunted him. I said, "Mr. H, I know how you feel about Jesus—that in your eyes He was a good man but not the Son of God. But I tell you He is real and truly loves you, and

He really is God's Son who loved you so much He gave His life for you and the world. He died for you and me so we can have eternal life and never be alone. You will have no reason to be afraid to die or see that black hole again. Jesus is alive and well and will never leave you or forsake you when you leave here." He was truly listening to me. Whenever we were alone, I gave him words of assurance that he didn't need to be afraid. God was in control. I let the Holy Spirit guide me in what to say and never forced anything upon him.

One night, the night nurse was to come in at 9:00 p.m., but she called and said she would be late and wouldn't be there until 10:00 p.m.

It was as if someone spoke to me and prompted me to get up out of my chair and talk to Mr. H right then. That still, small voice of God spoke to me and said, "This is the appointed time to speak to him. His time is growing short." So I did.

Mr. H hadn't taken that confession of faith yet, but I knew he was ready. I said, "Mr. H, I know you still worry about that black hole. You don't ever have to see or worry about it again if you truly believe that Jesus died for you and saved you from going into total darkness forever."

And for the first time in his life he whispered the words, "What should I do to have Jesus in my heart?"

Oh happy day! I read him 1 John about what a person must do to be saved and then John 3:16. He listened and was very sincere. That night, he gave his heart to Jesus, repeating after me the sinner's prayer.

During the days Mr. H had left, the morphine made him restless, so I sang to him. I got right up to his head and wrapped my arms around him and sang to him this song,

> Rest me, Jesus, for a while like
> you have so many times.
>
> Keep my safely in the eye of the storm.
>
> Gentle breezes on my face,
>
> Cares of life all erased, rest me Jesus
> in your strong and gentle arms.
>
> Rest me, Jesus, just once more, when
> the storms around me roll.
>
> Keep my safely in your strong and gentle arms,
>
> And when I get there on that shore, rest
> me, Jesus, just once more; Help me reach
> you on that golden shore. Jesus, dear
> Jesus, I'm ready to meet you I know."

He died peacefully as I sang this song to him.

In his final hours, I made sure he was shaved and had a nice shirt on. I asked his daughter to pick it out and applied his cologne. He would leave this life with dignity.

Mrs. H managed very well with her emotions. She would sit beside him on his bed and reminisce. She would gently stroke his face and cheeks and would thank him for such a wonderful life together. Then she called him her silver fox.

I had to walk out of the room to refrain from crying; I pulled myself together and then went back into the room.

On February 12, Mr. H passed very peacefully.

They had had a fairytale wedding and a happy married life for more than fifty years. What peace Mrs. H has now, knowing that she will see her love again beyond the gates of glory.

✝

Chapter 16

After Mr. H died, I met a new client named Mr. B His wife was a real spitfire. She was full of energy and involved in many activities and volunteered a lot in church groups as well.

Mr. B was a large, Italian man and had bladder cancer. He and his wife lived on the southeastern coast of Connecticut, where most of my clients lived. He and his wife were very Italian. She cooked all the traditional dishes and canned a lot. She made her own sauces and pasta from scratch. They also made their own homemade wine from the dark purple grapes that hung from vines over trellises. It reminded me of the Italian and French neighborhood I grew up in.

Mr. B did plumbing and heating work. He knew Nelson White, a famous artist, and his family. I had cared for his housemaid about ten years back. He and his wife lived right on the ocean front on a huge estate. He always smoked a fat cigar and wore a velvet smoking jacket whether it was winter or summer. He also worked for the fire department and was a big card player. They all got together at the firehouse with the wives as well and played cards. He read the newspaper from front to back and was a man of few words but a nice man.

He and his wife had no children.

He didn't live very long—three months.

I remember him telling me when I was leaving for Vermont that he was going to miss me. I almost fell over, because he was so quiet. He did love the Lord, and he was ready to go. It was very hard moving him around in his house and bed, because the rooms were so small. But through it all, his wife, came to know Christ as her Savior. We would open up and read the *Our Daily Bread* booklet and a scripture or two from the Bible. We would say a prayer together, and that would start our day. After Mr. B died, we stayed in touch, and she did very well on her own.

It was about a year later that I received a phone call from Mr. and Mrs. H's daughter once again.

Chapter 17

I often went to Connecticut to visit friends and would stop in and visit Mrs. H. We would go to dinner and to a movie. Sometimes, I would sleep over at her beautiful home. She had narcolepsy and would fall asleep at the drop of a hat. She had it almost all her life.

She was now eighty-four years old and would sleep a lot. This was happening even when her husband was alive and I was caring for him.

Her daughter would stop by and find her asleep sitting on a bench or the trashcan in her kitchen. Mrs. H also had a shunt at the base of her skull, and that was to keep fluid away from her brain. I always said if she ever needed me, I would come down. They asked me if I would come down and care for her and stay right at the house with her. I said yes. She was very special to me, and we got along so well.

I arrived after Thanksgiving on a Sunday. Since I had been there before, I knew Mrs. H's routine, and there were no problems with us living together.

The first thing I concentrated on was her edema. He legs

were extremely swollen and had openings that would weep. I put warm compresses on her legs with her feet elevated.

I applied sterile gauze on them and wrapped her legs up with an ace bandage to stop the swelling. After three weeks, her legs were completely healed. Her specialist was very impressed and said he had never seen her legs healed up in all her years.

I placed special ointment on them at night to help them get better. She was very glad; so was her daughter.

Every day, we went out for a ride and went shopping as well. She loved going out. She was such a lady and fun to be with. She would call a skunk a "wood pussy," and if she had diarrhea, she would say she had "the green-apple quickstep!" We went to a grocery store called Stop and Shop, and she called it Pause and Purchase. She had a special ice-cream cup she called her PC cup. It stood for portion control. If she had to run to urinate, she would say, "I have to dash with dignity." She had another saying: "Men perspire, horses sweat, but women *glow.*"

She had the philosophy that if you're upset, you should never say anything you would regret but should stop and think what to say.

She was such fun, and we often laughed together.

I took her to several functions that she was invited to—a book club, a museum Christmas party—and I was invited to them all with her because I was her nurse. They were all very gracious.

The church she belonged to also had a big Christmas party after services on a Saturday night. It was very nice. They served champagne and several lovely dishes of holiday foods that the congregation brought in. Mrs. H always brought in a few bottles of wine.

At Christmastime, I would take Mrs. H and we would go riding around to look at Christmas lights all over New London. We also set up her pre-lighted tree and lights for the windows. I went to the basement with her to bring the things upstairs.

We decorated the house before she was to depart for Georgia to spend two weeks with her daughter. She didn't want to go. She sensed that her children were making arrangements to remove her from her house, not because she need special care but because they wanted to sell the house for the profits they would gain. This saddened Mrs. H. Her children had not accepted the Lord, so they did not see the blessings and privileges they had received growing up. They only saw value in monetary things and had become selfish. They did not believe what God said—that we are to honor our mothers and fathers.

Mrs. H said, "The kids can take me out feet first before I leave my home!" This was the home her loving husband had bought her in the neighborhood where she grew up. It was more than a building.

Before Mrs. H left, she said, "Promise me you'll return to me."

"I promise; I will be back," I said.

Chapter 18

I received a phone call from the daughter after Christmas the time when Mrs. H was due back and I was to return. She called to tell me they had told their mom I wanted to remain in Vermont and was not returning. I was devastated that her daughter had told her that lie. How dare they treat their mother with such disrespect? I cried for a week.

When Mrs. H left, she told me, "I will miss you!"

I told her I would be with her till she no longer wanted me.

She said, "That will never happen! I love you."

I said, "The same here."

I heard God's still, small voice saying to me, "Be still and know I am God. I will take care of this in due season."

I'm sure that Mrs. H was upset and hurt that she thought I had left her, but I know since her passing to be with the Lord she knows the truth. In March 2011, she had a stroke and died three days later. I was never told Mrs. H had passed. They never had the decency to call. I saw the obituary in the newspaper. I wish every one of my stories had a happy ending, but that wouldn't be true. As a hospice nurse, you see the good, the bad, and the ugly, but what we really need to remember is that in whom we place our trust and how we walk this life and treat others is what matters. We need not to allow Satan to get a foothold in our lives.

I will always remember her and our special times together. She and her husband will always be special to me, and one day we will meet again in heaven.

I passed by the home one night after Mrs. H had passed, and all the lights were on. They had workers in to get it ready for sale. How sad to see. She loved her home so much.

Their mother has always been there for her children, and they have had the best in life that anyone could have. Money can have a positive or negative effect on a person. It all depends on if they allow the money to control them and make it their god. If it does, greed will set in, and that person's heart will turn cold.

I found the same thing with one of the daughters of the patient I had. She wanted me to stop feeding her mother so she can die faster. What a terrible thing! She said it's time to stop; her mother has been lingering long enough. Her mother was in good health even though she was bedridden. Not all her children are like that.

Chapter 19

Meme was a wonderful, kindhearted person to me. She always placed Russell Stover chocolates for me on her dresser that no one was allowed to touch but me.

When the other hospice nurses stopped in, she would say, "The chocolates are for Ditty." (It was the nickname she gave me.)

As a hospice nurse, it's very hard when a person dies, because we are left to mourn on our own; we have no one to comfort us. We do have counselors, but we never get time to see them, as we are too busy going to new patients.

Meme was raised in Boston and lived next door to Rose Fitzpatrick Kennedy. They were playmates, rivals, and friends. When Meme got older, she met her husband and dated. He knew many politicians and would tell me stories about them all. Sometimes he would give me the inside scoop on the inner workings of a political family.

He knew Tip O'Neal. He got his start in the political arena because of the Kennedys. Meme settled down with her husband in Philadelphia, and he was a top manager for Sears. She belonged to the garden club and loved gardening.

She was going to radiation therapy every day when the cancer really took hold. The treatments made her so very sick when she returned home with her husband. I would meet them at the car, and she would be lying down in the backseat throwing up in her small trashcan.

Poor thing—she was always very thin and frail, and this didn't help her.

I remember when her sister had to come visit her. She and her sister were always at odds, always competing and outdoing one another. She was bedridden at this time and wanted her hair colored before her sister saw her. Meme was very vain. It was funny.

So I had her husband go to the pharmacy to get her hair color. I set up a large garbage bag and placed it on her pillow and made a funnel-like drain for the water to run off. I placed a trashcan by the bed and then proceeded to color her hair, wash it, and then set it. It worked out really well. I put makeup on and then applied lipstick. We put a pretty, white, flannel-lined satin nightgown on her with a nice ruffle around her neck. She looked like a little doll.

She was thrilled to see herself in the mirror and was satisfied and ready to see her sister.

The visit went well, and that was the last time they were together. Three weeks later, Meme passed. She and her husband had been married over fifty years.

She had given me a lovely vase that had been given to them when they were married. It's tall and has a grosgrain ribbon finish. To this day, I treasure it. I've always had a sentimental side and never part with gifts from my patients or family.

It was a very sad time for her husband, as they had been very close. She never suffered and didn't need a lot of comfort care medications to keep her pain free. She was amazing.

One thing I did notice with Meme was that she took great pride in her gardening club. She lived in Germantown, Philadelphia. She always had women over for her teas and liked playing the part. Her husband pampered her, and they had money to enjoy the finer things in life. Her husband was a golf player, and he would join his friends and have a few cocktails.

It's not always easy saying good-bye to those you have cared for. I always call the family a week or two after their loved one's passing to make sure they are okay and reminisce about that person and how special they were. It's never easy, but it's important to me for there to be closure for the family and me as well. God and the Holy Spirit seem to give me the necessary love and knowledge of what to say.

If a person has no compassion for their patients or the families, then they are in the wrong line of work. Jesus encouraged us to visit those in prison, care for the sick, and feed the poor. It takes love, kindness, compassion, and lots of patience. It can be emotionally draining but very rewarding.

✚
Chapter 20

Mrs. S had ovarian cancer. She was financially well off, but you would never have known it. They owned the largest junkyard and parts business in the area. Her husband and she lived in a simple house with no frills. They spent their down time motorcycle riding and belonged to a motorcycle club. They were very close and had five children.

They were a rowdy French family and liked to drink.

They always had a closet full of hard alcohol and plenty of money lying around, and they liked to have fun.

She was an unusual case; she had had stage five-breast cancer for fourteen years. Her children didn't know in all the years she had it. She wanted to keep them from worry and continued to work in her herbal garden and read her Bible each day and spend time with her Savior.

In the final days of her illness, she got weaker and weaker. Then she broke the news to her children after seeing her doctor. She never suffered pain in all her years. God protected her from that.

The last week, she was so weak she took to the bed, and that was when I was called. The family was exhausted and needed our help.

She wasn't able to get out of bed at all. She wasn't in a hospital bed, so it was difficult to do her care with her bed so low to the floor. She was a tiny person, and her daughter told me how much she loved her gardens with all sorts of herbs. She had numerous books about herbs and calendars. She also had wonderful vegetable gardens. I never got to speak to her about these interests of hers; I would have loved to learn a lot about gardening from her. She was in her final days and hours when we met.

The nurse they had wasn't much of one, and that was when I was called in. I was just filling in that day, because her regular nurse had the day off.

I noticed that she had brown skin, which I thought was from an old tan. But it wasn't! It was dirt that never had been scrubbed off.

I gave the family an order to purchase for me some supplies for their mother—Buff Puffs to do her skin, a razor to shave her legs, and lotion and oil to do her body and keep the skin to moist.

The nurse had neglected her. She wasn't fit to be called a nurse. I like to do the care that I would want done for myself or my loved ones. I try to place myself in someone else's shoes.

Well, in no time her skin was in tip-top shape. That was the start of our relationship and my caring for Mrs. S.

She was very sick and confused from the high doses of drugs she had to have to manage the pain. She was on morphine. She had just turned fifty-four; I brought her a rose and baby's breath for her birthday. She was so confused in her drug-induced state that she thought the rose was a microphone and thought she was on *Let's Make a Deal,* a TV show she loved and watched every day.

I shared the love of God with her and told her how Jesus loved her. She gave her heart to Jesus before she died at the twelfth hour. Her son was taking his mother's sickness very hard.

He just couldn't understand why she had to die this way and found it very difficult to handle it. What was upsetting to him was that his parents had been planning on traveling a lot, and now their dreams were shattered. They had saved and saved, and now the dream was over. There were many problems with alcohol and drugs among the siblings, but one thing was for sure: the whole family was supportive and there for each other and their parents, which was very nice.

Chapter 21

Mrs. W was a sweet person. I remember her having a Bible in each room, sometimes two. She had many devotionals and was a true servant of God. She read every day. She spoke very softly to me; her voice had gotten weak.

Her daughter worked all day at General Dynamics, and her son lived across the street, but it was too hard for them. No one had any idea how to care for her except for her daughter-in–law, who was a nurse. It was very hard for them to see their mom in the dying process.

They needed our help desperately. Hospice of Southeastern Connecticut refers us as well as the hospitals. We have a spotless record as Christian women doing hospice privately.

She never showed her doctor or shared with her family the extent of her cancer until she couldn't hide it any longer.

Her disease ate up all her left side, inside and out.

The sight was very hard to take in. She had one huge, thick scab that covered her whole left side to her waist and under her arm.

It was amazing how she never had any pain in that site. It was not until the final two days of her life that she needed to be medicated with morphine.

God certainly protected her from pain all those years.

I often read her Psalm 91. It was her favorite Psalm. As things progressed, she didn't respond much, but I knew she could hear me. I anointed her with oil and asked Jesus to usher her into heaven; she had been a faithful servant of His.

The following night, I was there at 10:00 p.m., and she died at 11:15.

She went very peacefully and never struggled. She just fell asleep in Jesus.

I came over and dressed her and made her up so her husband could view her before the coroner came. Her husband was afraid to look at her, thinking the worst, but I encouraged him, saying that she didn't look the way he might think. He did very well when he went in with me to see her. She looked like she was just asleep. I want to make sure even in death a person has dignity.

I called her daughter to tell her, and they came right down.

I stayed till 2:00 a.m. The daughter handed me a check for the time, and I tore it up. I told her I didn't want to be paid. If I couldn't help them for free, I wasn't worth much. Staying with the family till the wee hours was a devotion of love, not a devotion to work and money.

As a caring, Christian woman, I would not have left a good testimony for my Lord if I had taken the money.

Her daughter later on gave me a beautiful pair of gold heart earrings she wanted me to remember her and her mother by.

She removed them from her ears and gave them to me. I was very touched. I am very blessed with good people, and sharing God's love is so important. I still run into her now and then.

Three months later, her husband had died. He was supposed to have a liver transplant and was in Boston Massachusetts General Hospital. He called me the night before his liver transplant. He was brokenhearted over the loss of his wife. I said a prayer with him and asked that the Lord bring him peace. That next morning, he died. He never made it into surgery. He never had a will to live after his wife died. I was supposed to care for him after surgery when he got back home to Vermont, but he never made it.

Chapter 22

I want to share with you about a dear nephew I had. His name was Robert. He was accomplished in his life and successful in so many ways.

He was a gold medalist in dance competitions all around the globe. He did ballroom dancing, tango, and much more.

He had written a couple novels and modeled for *Men's Vogue*. He had his own upscale salon in Houston, Texas. He catered to the wealthy. He was a master sculptor in hair and studied under Vidal Sassoon and Paul Mitchel. The salon was beautiful; it was done in marble and French provincial furniture. He did a lot of hair for celebrities. He did Reba's hair and received a signed autograph from her and also others.

We were very close, he and I. I miss him so much.

One weekend I went to New Jersey with Suzanne, who is a friend of mine, to visit her parents. On our way home to Vermont, I received a call. It was Robert. He thought he had the flu and wasn't getting over it. He had had it for a couple weeks with no change. He said he just couldn't seem to get rid of it. I asked him what the doctor had said.

I told him to get another opinion, and he said he had and they were running tests.

He called me a week later and gave me the sad news that he

had gallbladder cancer. I was shocked and upset to hear this, as we were so close. They gave him six months to live, because it had spread to the liver.

He was getting treatments in Niagara Falls that were supposed to be the best for treating the cancer. Wrong! It just made him sicker. He decided to take his pain meds, and when he went back home, he went on hospice.

He wanted to come and see me in the worst way. He loved going out and spending time at the house and also the cottage at Lake Champlain.

He knew this trip to visit me would be his last. His friend drove him to Vermont for the week. He had to lie down in the backseat with pillows and a blanket. I got him into the house, and he lay down with my little dog, Monty, which he loved.

I gave him the most wonderful time. My friend Suzanne and I took him to the state fair; we had barbecues with lobsters, steamers, and all kinds of wonderful summer foods for him; and we had bonfires with roasted marshmallows. He had a great time. We prayed each evening together, which he looked forward to. When he came, he brought me some old family pictures that my mother had once had. Then my sister had them, and my Robert wanted me to have them before he died.

I was happy. He made me promise to keep them, and only my daughter, Rose, was to have them and share them with my son, Paul.

He also gave me a beautiful picture he had done professionally.

I have it hung in my parlor and will forever treasure it.

When he got home, he took a turn for the worse.

I got a call from him, and he was weak and said, "I could use you now, Aunt Dottie, to care for me." I told him I would go take care of him. The nurse called me almost right after Robert called me. She said, "If you want to see your nephew, come now. He has little time left."

Chapter 23

I went with Suzanne, and she helped me drive the twelve hours to his home in Jamestown, New York, where he had retired from Houston, Texas.

When I got there, he already had slipped into a drug-induced coma. I took over taking care of him. I took care of him for two days. I washed him, medicated him, and sang him "Rest Me Jesus." The song always seems to give my patients peace. I bathed him, gave him his medication, and explained the care I was giving him as I did each part of his care.

I spoke gently in his ear of the Love of Jesus and how God loved him very much and how he was going to see Him pretty soon.

I was saddened that his mother never came to say her good-byes to her son.

She thanked me for caring for him.

God can challenge us in any way He wants to.

I talked to her and explained how he died and told her that

he had gone peacefully. Robert (our family called him Bob) wrote in his eulogy about me,

> I would like to mention a special and very precious person I love very much and who has been a great part of my life these past couple years. Having been privileged to have her not only in my life but as a relative, this is a woman that works tirelessly and endlessly, pleasing people without a complaint or asking for anything in return. She has been there for me when nobody else was, believed in me, always encouraged me to go forward, would help me stay in line with my own spirituality, and again asked for nothing in return. To me personally, she is my guardian angel, a person to aspire to and emulate in our own lives on a daily basis. She is my beautiful, red-headed Aunt Dottie.

I just burst out crying. I was taking his death hard as it was, and for him to say this took me by surprise.

I never expect anything in return for what I do. I do it all for God's glory. We just need to be still and know that he is God.

Two weeks before he died, Robert gave me a Waterford Crystal Angel and said he wanted me to have it. I knew after he died why he intended it for me. After his eulogy was read, I understood.

He was only fifty-four years old when he died. I have the reassurance that I will see him again in glory.

Chapter 24

I want to say I am thankful for all the memories I have. I want to say I hope that each one of us has a story to tell and to give God the glory for what God has allowed us to do for Him in His service in this earthly life.

I have had only one bad experience with a family while working in hospice. The patient himself was a sweet, kind man who had cancer and Alzheimer's as well.

The wife had a bitter spirit and always liked causing trouble in her family. Satan certainly had a hold in that household.

It was a home of drugs and alcohol. Her daughter was an alcoholic and was always after her mother's jewelry.

Mr. J had been a jeweler all his life and had purchased beautiful jewelry for his wife, which was quite valuable.

The daughter would come in and ransack the house to get all the jewelry. The mother would give it to her and then say she had stolen it. Satan can cause harm in many ways, despite Christians that are serving these people.

The house had an evil presence about it. I had a dream one

night that there were rats crawling all over the house. It was dark in the dream. The next day, I was watching a Christian program, and they mentioned that if a person has a dream about rats, it indicates demonic influence. I was meant to see that program.

I don't care to remember that place at all; it was a nightmare from hell. But I do like remembering Mr. J, who was such a sweet man and patient. He suffered plenty, and my work partner and I had to stay on top of his pain to manage it. He had problems with his lungs and had smoked some in his early years.

He was sick for about two months. Then his body started failing fast. He loved for me to singing Jesus songs to him. He liked the nurses that came in. I worked a twelve-hour day shift.

I would talk to him a lot about his work and how Jesus loved him and how he would make a transition from earth to heaven any time now.

The day he left us, he was in a lot of pain, so we had to increase his medication to keep him as pain-free as possible.

His grandchildren would come in to see him. They loved him.

He never complained or said much. He loved the Lord and would say his prayers at the table.

He died midmorning with his grandchildren around his bed.

We contacted his daughter, and she wouldn't come down till the night before his funeral. When she did show up, she only came to get what she wanted first.

It was a grueling time in that terrible, dysfunctional home.

The drugs and all the kids going in and out of their home were terrible. They couldn't wait for the "old man" to die so they could get hold of his money and car.

The rest of the relatives said how bad they were.

We saw it for ourselves. I had to seek God's face before I even entered that home. As God's word says, "Take the shield of faith, with which you will be able to quench all the fiery darts of the wicked one" (Ephesians 6:16). "Therefore take on the whole armor of God, that you may be able to withstand in that evil day" (Ephesians 6:10–18).

It was a breath of fresh air to leave there. Mr. J was in a better place now.

Matthew 16:26 says, "For what is a man profited, if he gains the whole world, and lose his own soul?"

And Matthew 19:24 says, "And again I say unto you, it is easier for a camel to go through the eye of a needle, than for a rich man to enter into the kingdom of God."

I went back to my home to rest. It is a mental strain to make right decisions for the patient—watching, being on top of their care, dealing with family drama. And there are some that just touch your heart, and you feel the loss when they go.

It was the worst experience I ever encountered. All the care workers were relieved to leave there, but we kept them in our prayers. They needed it.

It was nice to be home and spend time with the family and my special little dog, Monty. He was born on the first of January 2005. I got him as gift when my grandson was being deployed to Ramadi Iraq. I named him after my state capital, Montpellier. Monty is a therapy dog and we have been members of the Therapy Digs of Vermont since 2006. He has won awards for obedience and beauty and not to add to his already growing awareness of how adorable he is, he has won Pet Idol of Vermont two years in a row!

✚ *Chapter 25*

My present patient, Mrs. M, loves my dog. He's a therapy dog, and when I'm home, we visit the children's hospital unit that houses almost all cancer patients or those suffering from some other serious sicknesses.

My patient's family is very special and has encouraged me to bring Monty with me to stay at her home.

At present, I have been with Mrs. M for two years. This is unusual, because usually they are with us six months or less. But one thing is for sure: they don't go anywhere until God decides to call them—not one minute before.

Mrs. M was born in New Zealand and lived the privileged Victorian life. Her father was in the cargo-shipping business, import and export. She has said she didn't know why she had been so fortunate to live such a regal life of privilege, but she had. She's very thankful. She is a humble person, and you would never know she came from a life of wealth.

At ninety years old, she decided she had had enough and wanted to cut off all doctors' treatments and medications and wanted to die. She decided she was old enough and it was time to leave this life. She is very unique. We love her British accent. She can make us laugh; we never know what she will say next. She was playmates with Queen Elizabeth!

Her aunt and uncle had a castle next door to the Queen Mother, Mary. Anne, her cousin, was chosen as a lady in waiting in Queen Elizabeth's coronation in 1953. They were childhood friends. Mrs. M attended the coronation along with her parents and siblings, one brother and one sister. She is very interesting to talk with.

She and her husband have a cargo-shipping business as well that has been in the family since Mr. M's great-grandparents had it. They ship oil all over the world. She has shared with me how the great-grandparents had tall steamships that had big sails. When there wasn't the wind to carry them, they had the steam. She commented to me, "That's why you see so many paintings of sailboats and ocean steamships in our home." Of course, they're all original paintings. She is not one to brag.

Mr. M knew Aristotle Onassis. He couldn't stand him; he never trusted him and said he wasn't honest. I'm sure his comment was because they were in a competitive business.

Mrs. M traveled all around the world many times with her husband on business. They always had a maid, who also served as a nanny to the children.

Mrs. M always treated her help well, and I asked her one day why she hired mostly African American people. She replied that she wanted to give them a chance in life. She is always gracious and open to helping others and is very aware of those working for and helping her. She is always concerned that they don't get overtired. She's forever telling me, "Now, Dottie, please sit down now and get off your feet; you're working too hard!" She is just a doll to have for a patient.

I mentioned to her that she is so full of history in her life. She said to me, "Well, I guess there is more to come!" She always has an answer for everything.

She was telling me about her father's cargo-shipping business in New Zealand. It was import and export. He shipped everything in general.

During the war, her father loved beer and still was able to special order it from Germany as well as cigars—that is, until Britain took their ships to fight the Germans. They were returned after the war. She told me how her father had to start over and rebuild the ships. Of course, they weren't in the same shape as when the government took them. They were dirty and in dire need of repair. There was very little money after the war. Most of New Zealand and other British countries had to start over from scratch, including her mum and dad.

✚
Chapter 26

Mrs. M met her husband through her sister and sister's friend, who arranged for them to meet. That was the beginning of their courtship. They dated two years and then married, and while Mr. M finished serving in the World War II, she went to California to live with his aunt and said they were very gracious to her the whole time she lived with them. When Mr. M returned home, they moved to New York City and took over the cargo-shipping business from his parents.

When I met Mrs. M, She was very angry that she was not going to die when she had planned she would. She thought she could just get a large dose of morphine and be done with life. I mentioned that this was out of her hands. The rich have a sense of controlling everything in their lives, because they have the power to control most things. She didn't know God, and she never read the Bible and didn't have one in her home. Some wealthy people give no thought to what they believe in and where they are going when they die. Money is their god.

I explained to her that my job is to save lives and bring comfort and care, not to take lives. She was angry with God and asked, "Why am I still here? I want to go now. I lived a very privileged life, and now I want it to be over. I don't want to live this way."

I told her it just was not her time yet. God wasn't finished with her and would teach her patience. His timing is different in His realm then in ours, and His reasoning is not our way of thinking.

I continued to share the love of God with her, took care of her as Christ would have me do, and had many conversations about where our eternal home is and where our treasure is truly stored. I let her know God is our creator and we must know Him personally and accept Him while there is still time.

The family treated me very well, and I became part of the family. I continued to show them kindness as well as the love of God and His Holy Spirit in me. I didn't act differently with them than with anyone else because of their financial status.

In time, Mrs. M found the Prince of Peace and asked Jesus into her heart.

She doesn't worry about her life and dying anymore. She is happy and does not complain about leaving. She now says, "I'm an old woman now at ninety-one years of age. I'm ready to die when God wants me." We now read daily devotions, and she likes that. "Isn't it wonderful I shared the love of God with you?" She agrees. We have had wonderful talks about the streets of purest gold and the beautiful gates that are one solid pearl. She can't imagine it. She smiles, and it brings her the peace that only He can give that surpasses all understanding. One evening, we were talking about heaven and what it will be like and whether we will look old or young when she said,

"One thing is for sure—Mr. M won't have a temper anymore. If he does, I'll kick him to another cloud!" How funny is that! I said, "And I won't be fat anymore." She said, "No, just covered." I laughed.

Sometimes, Mrs. M can get confused, but when we talk about our Lord, there is amazing clarity of heart and mind.

Chapter 27

She's amazing; she is so comical. We had a blackout when Hurricane Irene hit us in August 2011. We were out of power for a week, but we managed okay. I had candlelight for her dinners and used candlelight for her relaxed time of having wine.

(For the sake of any men who are reading my book—and ladies, you know what I will be referring to—and so there is an air of dignity to Mrs. M's story, the following subject will be discussed using the euphemism, "the girls.")

She mentioned that the girls always had been small and wished they were bigger. She said they were small as peanuts. I think the wine had gotten the best of her. Only half a glass! She was hysterical. "I wish I had your size. I was cheated!" she said. I told her it was because she had lost so much weight. "You look fine," I replied. "I could arrange to share mine with you. Then we would be even!"

"Oh no! I'm too old now, but do you know they have surgical procedures they do now for that?"

I laughed. "What would I do without you, Auntie?"

I had started calling her that. I said I was going to adopt her as an aunt since I had never had one that was special. "Well," she said, "Now you've got one!" So now she is Auntie to me.

What I like about my patients is that they put their trust in us and always confide and tell us their inner thoughts that they don't share with their families.

Through that hurricane, she was a real trooper about having no power. I had to make sure my nursing notes were finished before dark. I would read to her by candlelight, and we would reminisce about my time growing up and her life growing up.

I had a regular routine each day with her without power. It was hard at times, but we managed. She made it easy because of her sweet disposition and patience. She found it to be fun. We had so many great times of sharing.

We were blessed to have hot and cold running water all the time. Some buildings had none at all, but there was no problem with giving her a daily bath plus washing at bedtime. After seven days, the power came on. "Thank God!" I was speaking to her daughter, and I yelled out, "The Lord has mercy!"

She said, "What's wrong?"

"The power just came on!" I exclaimed. It was 8:30 p.m. Praise God!

It's amazing what you can't do without power. God has His way of teaching us patience and teaching us to put our trust in Him in times of trouble.

It was nice having quiet times to read and study the Bible. I enjoyed that. I read to Auntie each day. In the evening, I read her a novel. I asked if she minded it. "Not at all; I love it!" She truly is amazing. If someone were to ask me who my hero is, I would have to say Mrs. M. She has taught me so much in the two years I have been with her.

She's classy, regal, a real lady, and gracious in all she says and does. She is very dignified, very polite, soft spoken, and never raises her voice.

She has become very Christ like in heart and mind.

I will truly miss her and all there is about her when she dies.

She also has a dry sense of humor. Just the other night, she passed gas, and I pretended to be shocked. She chuckled, and I said, "What was that?"

And in her proper British accent, she replied, "Well, it's just me shooting bunnies!"

One day after lunch, she had a vision of her husband who had passed on and said, "There he is!"

I said, "Who?"

She replied, "It's my husband, He is standing in an elevator at the foot of the bed motioning me to come with him."

I asked her, "Well, do you want to go?"

She gave it some thought and said, "No, not really."

So I told her, "Tell him to go!"

She looked at me and said, "You tell him to go!"

So I said, " Auntie says she is not ready to go; you need to go back! And off he went, back in the elevator with the other people who were waiting. She said that in her country they believe that when a person is dying, you must open the window to let their spirit take flight to where they are going. So I told her I wasn't going to allow that just now. "Not yet, my dear, because I would miss you too much," I said, and God knows how much I would miss her.

Chapter 28

On December 8, 2011, she turned ninety-one, and I made sure she had a very special birthday.

One of her daughters came for the weekend before her ninety-first birthday and spent most of the day with her and came back the next day to bring her a few gifts. Her other daughter in California came for two days. Her son, who lives in Connecticut, came to visit. She was very happy and had several well-wishers call as well. Her brother in New Zealand spoke to her. She was surprised to hear his voice. "Oh, I thought you flew the coop!"

He chuckled and said, "No, I'm still here."

She thought he had passed away. He is ninety-six years old. I bought her a lovely bouquet of white lilies and red roses with holly to make it very festive for her. It may be her last Christmas, and I wanted it to be special. I also got her a birthday cake, not too big but a little one for her. A hospice aide that comes in each day to bathe her brought her a homemade chocolate almond bundt cake. She was so delighted.

I also decorated her home with a tree and outdoor lights and did the inside as well. It was just beautiful, and she just loved it. Christmas music played in the background for her as well.

A gift from her daughter was on its way, a CD of Handel's *Messiah* for us to play. She said that is her favorite.

Any time I went home to Vermont, I would call her. I would bring her back some maple products from there, which she loves and looks forward to each time I would return.

One evening while I was changing her and repositioning her, she told me, "You know what? I bet you can't see your own butt standing there."

I never had given it thought. I said, "Matter of fact, you're right!"

So she responded, "Well, that's okay. I'll watch out for your behind, and you watch mine!" She is always ladylike. She is so funny. We have a lot of laughs.

When Auntie gets sad and misses her large home, I say her mansion is in heaven. It won't even compare to the home she had here, which was a mansion. "Just think, Auntie—streets of purest gold. You can't beat that!" She'd smile and then say she felt better.

I cannot say that I blame her for feeling down at times. She is bedridden, needs total care, and has to be fed. She's not looking forward to how long she can be this way. But I tell her God isn't finished with her yet. She's a very wise woman, and I take all her advice seriously. God has certainly blessed me with the job, and winning her to Christ and also just learning from her has been a great benefit for me. She hasn't been successful for nothing, and I also believe that God has a certain path He puts us on in this life. Why are some so wealthy when others have to work so hard and struggle?

I believe that we ourselves bring some of it on. We need to look for God's direction and also listen to His still, small voice regarding what He wants for us. Sometimes we just don't seek Him or even listen to that voice. When he speaks, we can know, as He gives us that strong sense of intuition. We should pay attention to our instincts and the Holy Spirit that guides us.

I know God will call her home one day. For me, I will have mixed emotions. I will be sad, because I will miss her, but I will have joy in my heart that she is no longer confined to her mortal body and is free from sickness and able to rest in the loving arms of her Savior. I know one day we will be reunited again and never say good-bye. Just think—together forever shooting bunnies! I can see you smiling, Auntie!

You're always a proper British lady.

Epilogue

We are ambassadors for Him, the salt of the earth, a lighthouse for the world, a lifeline of loving others, because God is love.

The nice thing about hospice is we are there to encourage the patients, give them lots of love and tender care, and guide them spiritually. This is where I come in. I'm not the average person, I know. I go all the way for my patients and spoil them and treat them as if they were my own. That is my calling—to do God's work in the end stages of life.

I'm on my mission for Christ when I leave Vermont to head out of state to care for someone whose time is very limited.

It's getting closer to His return; we need to make our time count. I refuse to sit around and let someone do the work when there is so much I can use my gift to do.

If we all do our part as we live here till we are called home, God will reward us for all our work we have done for His glory.

"Do you know where you are going? When this earthly life is past?

Will the seed that you are sowing bring a harvest that will last?"

We sow the seed; God produces the harvest.

I want to leave a legacy so that all remember me for what I have done for others, and hopefully I have touched many lives as they have touched mine.

CPSIA information can be obtained at www.ICGtesting.com
Printed in the USA
LVOW06s2241030714

392736LV00001B/57/P